Advance Praise for *Museum Strategy and Marketing:*

"*Museum Strategy and Marketing* isn't the new jargon. It's a new set of probing questions about museum purpose, structure, and operations by authors in touch with both museum realities and business school approaches. Museum boards and directors will be interested in *Museum Strategy and Marketing* because Neil and Philip Kotler raise questions that they should be asking."

> —Philip M. Nowlen, assistant executive vice chancellor,
> University of California, Irvine

"The Kotler brothers have brought together the best of current museum strategic planning and marketing theory and practice in a book that will stimulate readers to begin working toward making their own institutions more successful in the marketplace."

> —G. Donald Adams, director of marketing,
> Automotive Hall of Fame

"As museums seek to expand their public dimension, this book serves as a powerful tool for all levels of management. The Kotlers have a keen sense of the diverse world of museums."

> —Alberta Sebolt George, president and CEO, Old Sturbridge Village

"*Museum Strategy and Marketing* is a fascinating blend of real-world experience in managing museums and classic business theory. The book offers thought-provoking models for both museum professionals and volunteer leadership."

> —David Mosena, president and CEO,
> Museum of Science and Industry, Chicago

"This comprehensive volume offers a primer for planners, a tool for marketers, and insights for trustees; it is a guide for building audiences, attracting donors, and enhancing the 'museum experience' for all constituencies."

> —Stephen A. Greyser, Richard P. Chapman Professor (Marketing
> and Communications), Harvard Business School, and marketing
> committee chair, Museum of Fine Arts, Boston

"A must read for every museum director, executive, and trustee. Marketing orientation and strategy are key to the survival and growth of any museum. This book provides the needed blueprint."

> —Jerry Yoram Wind, the Lauder Professor and professor of marketing,
> The Wharton School, and trustee, The Philadelphia Museum of Art